SOLUTIONS
FOR THE PROBLEM
OF BODIES IN SPACE

Also by Catherine Barnett

Human Hours
The Game of Boxes
Into Perfect Spheres Such Holes Are Pierced

SOLUTIONS
FOR THE PROBLEM
OF BODIES IN SPACE

poems

Catherine Barnett

Graywolf Press

This publication is made possible, in part, by the voters of Minnesota through a Minnesota State Arts Board Operating Support grant, thanks to a legislative appropriation from the arts and cultural heritage fund. Significant support has also been provided by other generous contributions from foundations, corporations, and individuals. To these organizations and individuals we offer our heartfelt thanks.

Published by Graywolf Press
212 Third Avenue North, Suite 485
Minneapolis, Minnesota 55401

www.graywolfpress.org

Published in the United States of America

ISBN 978-1-64445-287-5 (paperback)
ISBN 978-1-64445-288-2 (ebook)

2 4 6 8 9 7 5 3 1
First Graywolf Printing, 2024

Library of Congress Control Number: 2023951380

Cover design: David Wells

Cover art: Ememem

CONTENTS

I.

II.

III.

SOLUTIONS
FOR THE PROBLEM
OF BODIES IN SPACE

I.

Studies in Loneliness, i

I understood I was alone, or that I wanted to be alone, right there in the middle of my big family, so I asked to move out of the room I'd shared with my two baby sisters into a spare room downstairs by the kitchen where I had for company not the sound of their breathing but of my father's prized ice machine dropping its tidy cubes automatically, all night long.

I had for company four doors, it was a room of doors—

—

When did loneliness become equal parts strategy, ministration, origin story, addiction?

—

At lunch one hot July day I said I love loneliness. That was summers ago—

—

New Year's Eve assignment: go out alone to a bar . . .

—

The main character in *Cast Away* befriends a volleyball. This is one signature of a lonely person—the personification of objects.

Rarely do I practice this but somehow, without realizing it, I have given my car a female pronoun, I spread blankets across her roof when it hails.

—

And how to answer my mother as we brush her hair, drive her car:

"Does a human being ever run out of questions?"

"Look at all those birds sitting in a row on the fence. Why do you think they like to be together?"

———

In one of my favorite Carson McCullers stories, an old man drinks beer in the morning. Abandoned by his wife, he grieves for five years until he learns the science of love, which is to start with objects—a tree, a rock, a cloud—and learn to love each one before trying to love a human being.

———

Last week someone placed an ad on Craigslist: "Anyone need a grandma for Christmas? I can cook dinner, will bring food and gifts."

Some people thought it was a hoax, some people told her to kill herself.

By the time a young man in Tulsa, Oklahoma, tried to find "the lonely grandma"—his own mother having recently died of cancer—she'd removed the post.

———

"At least 10% of schoolchildren report feeling lonely either always or most of the time."

I always begged my parents to wake me before they left.

———

An old friend gathers petals, leaves, twigs, and stones when she walks her dog. Every day she makes something out of what she found: "I was here."

Envoy

I was trying to look a little less like myself
and more like other humans,

humans who belonged, so I put on a skort.
Purchased in another life, when I had a husband

and wrote thank-you notes and held dinner parties,
the skort even had its own little pocket,

and the fingerprint stains yellowing the fabric
were almost invisible, nothing to be ashamed of

as I walked past homes and faces
with their welcome signs and their no-trespassing signs.

I was hoping to look domesticated,
or at least domesticable,

that I too could walk the trails
and then return home, stretch out

beside another human and watch something
on a big screen until it was time to sleep.

I too had veins at my wrist,
and I'd read Maslow,

with his hierarchy of needs.
I remembered that love and belonging

were pretty basic, and that at the top
of the pyramid was transcendence.

Late that night I took off the skort
and lay down on the kitchen floor of a house

where years ago a boy and his girlfriend
overdosed in the basement, a fact

I try not to remember.
There used to be a cross staked outside,

beneath the blue spruce that died
when the place was abandoned.

Because I am afraid,
I left the outside light on.

Halogen burns hot, so bright
it must have stunned the imperial moth

shimmering against the window screen.
Most moths would rather spin around lights

than mate, which is all they are put here to do,
and sometimes they just tire themselves out

flying at night. This one was disguised
as an autumn leaf, though it was only midsummer.

Size of my hand.
As much enigma as legerdemain,

very temporary,
at most she would live a week.

Something about the way she waited there,
wings outstretched, still as a flat lichened stone,

made me want to rescue my copy of Maslow
from the basement and study the hierarchy again.

In the diagram I saw sex at the very bottom—
along with eating, drinking, sleeping.

I wondered if that meant it was foundational,
or optional. The moth, vibrating there

in the circle of light, seemed to be choosing
transcendence over other basic needs.

Imperial moths have no mouthparts,
they don't eat, they make no sound.

In the morning, I buried her
under the ghost spruce as cars sped by.

Before I tossed the dirt back
over the shallow hole, I took a photo,

to prove there really was such a thing
as an imperial moth.

To prove she wasn't alone.
Wings made of iridescent chitin

arranged to look like leaf litter,
in the dirt she glowed a little.

Nicholson Baker & I

At dinner I was seated next to him,
with whom I might have fallen in love
were he not married and living in Maine.

"What's your favorite anthology?" he asked,
out of the blue. I told him I like
In the Shape of a Human Body I Am Visiting the Earth,

where even friends who dread poetry
find something to love, some gateway drug.
Which must be how we got to addictions.

"What are *you* addicted to?" he asked.
Not wine, I thought,
though our wine glasses were touching.

Not crab cakes, which I moved from my plate to his,
or dinner parties, though I wondered who he was,
this stranger in a navy sweater.

"Mornings," I said.
"Trader Joe's vegetarian meatballs," he said,
but he'd resigned himself to potatoes

and spoke of their virtues. Every morning
he boils up six or seven
and eats them all day long.

Perhaps because I wasn't wearing my glasses,
I mistook a hole in his sweater for a feather,
a small down feather on his shoulder,

and tried to remove it, but it was only a hole,
only something to be repaired,
and I'd embarrassed him.

He said he'd spend the rest of dinner
with his hand over the hole, like this,
and as he lifted his arm across his body

I noticed other holes, in the other sleeve,
and thought of all I've meant to mend.
Meant to mean.

I keep many drafts of failed poems
on my kitchen table, beside a little sewing kit,
a notebook, and this memory of Nicholson Baker,

whom I walked to the subway later that evening,
afraid he might get lost. "Wait a minute," he said.
We were in Times Square,

I was guiding him through the canyon of lights,
which were an antidote to grief,
as was Nicholson Baker himself,

someone I just chanced to meet
and may never see again.
"Don't look," he said as we were crossing Broadway.

"My pants are falling off."
So I looked instead at the fifty-five giant LED
nonstop life-affirming lights,

which made me think of my father,
sundowning 3,000 miles away.
Shouldn't we try to floodlight the dark

outside the dining room where he sleeps,
or doesn't sleep, in a hospital bed?
Flawed solutions are sometimes prayers.

"Open the second shutter
so that more light may come in,"
said Goethe on his deathbed.

It costs $25,000 a day to keep Times Square lit
but it wouldn't cost much to light up
our front steps. Failing that,

we keep giving my father morphine,
now that he is officially in hospice
and before we gain

the hour of daylight savings,
which he might not live to see.
I know how addictive it is.

Light.
Open the second shutter now.
I could have waited there indefinitely

while Nicholson Baker hiked up his trousers
and tried to keep his hand over the little feathery hole.
But we were on a journey of sorts, at a way station.

Which was where? And where were we headed,
Nicholson Baker and I?
I was heading home and he

to his overheated Airbnb,
which he chose, he said,
because it was near Alice's Tea Cup,

where once years ago he was served
a tea so electrifying it let him write
one good paragraph,

and he was looking for that high again.
He got out at 72nd Street.
At home later that night, I found him

in the pages of a slim, hilarious novel
whose hero lights a match
at the beginning of every chapter.

Studies in Loneliness, ii

I can't be lonely because there's not time—look at my calendar all booked up with the assuaging of loneliness.

—

Grace told me she sleeps with a mason jar!

—

I sleep in socks when I can't get warm. More and more I like to fall asleep and wake in a cold room, letting my solitary engine make its own heat.

The doctors snip the cord. I don't know if that's when it starts.

Itinerary

I cut my father's steak in small pieces
and read to him, who once read so beautifully to us.
Back out of all this now too much for us,
back when our father could repair anything,

it was as if he made us solely so we could stand there
and study him, listening to the Accutron
that hummed on his wrist as he measured.
We could see the insides of the watch,

and it would work, he told us,
in any gravitational field, at any speed.
It was so accurate—
99.9977% accurate—

Gordon Cooper said it saved his life
when something went very wrong
in his mission to circle the earth.
So there was nothing to fear

while our father drove Highway 1 at night
and the cliffs dropped to the Pacific
and we asked him to slow down
but he sped up.

Taillights swerved and flickered ahead.
Were they to start to fall, he said,
he'd just turn the other way.
I think I have been alarmed all my life.

Once, two or three martinis deep,
just beginning to lose his memory,
my father reached across the console
and whirled the steering wheel

right through my fingers.
Or did he put his foot on the gas?
Now the skin at my father's wrist is so thin
it bruises. I can almost see through it,

to all the mechanisms inside.
Dark blue bruises there, too.
I think he'd like a martini now—
lemon twist, no olive, I can hear him say—

but words have left him.
Have left him here, at the kitchen table,
where I listen to his new Timex
make no sound as the hours sweep by.

"Have You Ever Written a Poem about Death?"
My Mother Asks

We keep saying "it's ok it's ok it's ok"
to the improvisations sweeping through my father's body
like apnea,

like anaerobic gewgaw plumes radiating from what he is and was and is.
I can't know what it will be like when he's gone.
He's not Williams's "godforsaken curio" showing up

in the third draft of "Death."
That man there is my father.
This man here, right here.

Only in these last long years have I been able to comfort him,
I wouldn't have dared before, he distrusted comfort
and drank his coffee black to avoid the inconvenience of milk.

Now I can put my hand right here on his head.
And all I need to do is keep my face calm, a calm mirror
to his blank and seeking eyes.

That man there is my father.
This man here, right here.
I've used the word *hospice* before, without understanding,

just listening to the ad hoc hiss
and preternatural apneic sprinklers of childhood,
the dark green hose of

death feeding the extraordinary plumes.

Night Watch

"Don't worry, I will return," were not his dying words.
He had no dying words.

There was no pretense, no implosion.
11:00 p.m.

He was quiet, remote, dying,
sheer as a curtain.

The body is a big dumb object, he taught us.
Death is a genius.

"Do you understand?" he did not say.
11:05 p.m.

Still no protest.
Around him we were

a collective
for which there existed no name.

Vortex?
Hive? Enigma?

Astrophysicists were asking
for suggestions.

Terror. A terror of black holes,
someone proposed.

Yes, that was true.
Silence. A silence of black holes,

someone proposed.
That too was accurate.

What is metaphor?
What is metaphor for?

For you, my father,
genius in a big dumb object.

For when the curtains shivered
and we saw you enter the vortex

of world peace,
with its hive of enigmas.

Hyacinth

I think of him in his thinning white undershirt,
crisp white button-down, blue jeans,
and the red wool jacket that was a gift from my brother

who took my hand and placed it in my father's hand
before my father's hand was no longer my father's hand,
a hurried gesture, spontaneous, and full of my brother's kindness.

My brother was on watch. "Hurry," he'd said,
until he was surrounded by sisters.
We were all silent.

I don't know if my father forgave the years
I did not love him. Decades, even,
when I did not know I loved him.

Feels as if sorrow, like the highest shelves
at the dollar store I sometimes wander,
replenishes itself.

A month later, it was somehow April
in Washington State and a law was passed
that would have allowed us to place our father

in a vessel and surround him with wood chips
and straw, fungi and protozoa,
then let the compost age in an open-top

fifty-five-gallon drum until,
all seven brass-colored snaps
and two replaced hips sieved out,

he could have become soil for my mother's garden,
where the hyacinths, silent purveyors of sorrow
and forgiveness, might go forth and multiply.

Studies in Loneliness, iii

I take issue with all the studies saying beware loneliness, avoid loneliness, it will speed your death.

I say it will speed your death only if you believe it's a toxin.

Imagine loneliness is a drug curing you of loneliness! This is what I believe, on this late Friday morning before the dermatologist looks at me as if I were a carpet with stains.

―

I have to lie down in my sparkly pink G-string while she examines me for moles. She tells me I have calluses from sitting so much; she reminds me of the studies that show women who get Botox receive more positive reinforcement.

I tell her no thank you very much.

She says Botox could lower my raised eyebrow.

She says she doesn't give Botox to people who need to feel empathy, which I do, deeply, in order not to feel lonely.

At $500 a shot, Botox is an agent of loneliness.

―

I thought about beginning an essay with Aristotle's *Rhetoric*, and talking about the pathos, ethos, and logos of loneliness.

Or with the id, ego, superego—yes, that would be a way to think about it.

The id of loneliness—

Inductive loneliness? Deductive?

Studies in loneliness indicate that those high on the neuroticism scale are also high on the UCLA Loneliness Scale.

I think the existential danger of loneliness awakens the imagination, fuels it.

Who knows you best in the world?

Who knows me best are these black notebooks, purchased in bulk, used up one by one.

But you can't trust what you find here.

For example, sometimes I'm the Angel of Loneliness! Sometimes the Big Foot of Loneliness! Sometimes researcher, sometimes subject.

The sense of falling forever is one sign of loneliness, often the earliest sign.

"Vertigo," I say at the edge of the Grand Canyon, "I love the vertigo, it's calling to me."

Onto a plexiglass stand my son and I step into and above the void.

―

My mother finds her car by pressing the unlock button on the gadget and listening.

The Search

Left on the street in my mother's neighborhood:
children's games, utensils,
Ethical Theory, underlined

in blue ink:
"There are certain axiomatic truths . . .
expected to disappear from the earth."

But it's not like we don't know where my father's ashes are!
They're right upstairs, in his study,
where my mother dresses and undresses now.

And I can hear her hand on the banister,
sound of wind.
Soon we'll go back out, looking for my father's silver Avalon.

She can't remember where she parked it.
It's not in the cemetery we walk past
under trees full of summer fruit.

When I reach to pick one mulberry,
it comes attached to another. My mother
and I must also be looking for my father,

who turns out to have been soft and erasable,
like the #2 lead I use to write in my books,
some of which are my mother's books,

none of which were my father's.
I'd recognize their hands anywhere.

Untitled

"Isn't it dangerous to hold them in your mouth
like that?" I asked.

The steel T-pins pressed between my mother's lips
caught the light from the studio windows.

"Probably," she murmured.
"Probably," she says gently to questions I ask every day:

Are you hungry?
Did you sleep well?

Somehow I've been with her a week already,
the days passing like voices.

The probability of an event happening
is a number between zero and one.

One by one she removed the pins
and tacked up another drawing

that looked like a face, or a potato,
a homely potato edged with light.

Object study.
Vanitas.

To take back East with me
I chose a piece of painted plywood.

It didn't weigh much, I tucked it under my arm
as we walked slowly up the hill.

Neither of us asked the other
what to prepare, or how,

we just stopped at the market and wandered the aisles,
filling the basket with perishables.

It was getting late. I was in charge,
but I couldn't keep time from slipping away.

Dinner would be late again.
Who knows how long we were there,

my mother's beautiful lined face marked
with yellow, black, and red ochre

from a day's work. A life's work.
I unloaded the cart in a rush

and without thinking placed the painting
on the conveyor belt:

gold outline, central red omphalos,
unvarnished, unframed, unsigned.

The tomatoes and apricots ripened
imperceptibly as the cashier weighed them.

It was all happening so quickly, matrix codes
flickering under the high flickering lights

trained on whatever might get nicked.
"What's this?" the cashier asked.

She must have pressed a hidden button
that slowed the conveyor belt.

We stood for a moment in the middle
of anodyne space, nothing moving

except the old man carrying his bags
to the exit and the young families,

impatient, starting to fill their carts.
My mother once told me painters look backward

and forward at the same time. Since then
it's years and yet feels shorter than a day,

and I still don't understand. Or maybe
I do, yes, I cannot do otherwise.

Zero is looking backward.
One is looking forward.

Let me not stand here contemplating
the diminishing distance between them

but go on, go on with the story, such as it is,
there's still time, my flight isn't until tomorrow,

I'll wave until she's out of sight.
"What's this beautiful thing?" the cashier said again,

quietly, looking down at the painting
and then back up at us,

into my mother's face.
I think it will always be my mother's face.

Morning of Departure

The neighbor's mulberry tree spilling its fruit
onto the sidewalk stained the old sneakers
I took from my mother's closet, but there was no need
to steal, there's almost nothing you can ask for
that my mother wouldn't give you, except maybe
the bone from a T-bone steak—
she's a carnivore, like the coyote in the cemetery
where I walked each day in my mother's shoes.
It was so hot the asphalt buckled
and the cemetery crows kept their beaks open;
everyone except me was underground, staying cool.
From our respective shades, the solitary coyote
eyed me steadily, as if I belonged to her,
but all I wore was borrowed: the shoes, the skirt,
the clip holding my silver hair above my sweaty neck,
maybe even my own sweaty neck.
I'm not so dim not to know you can't take it with you
and still I wanted to keep my mother's shoes.
On the morning of my departure, I left a trail
of red-black mulberry juice that led into
and then out of her front door and down the steps
to the airport scanner where I untied the sneakers
and placed them carefully into the tray. By then,
my mother may already have forgotten I'd been to visit her.
"You're not leaving tomorrow, are you?" she kept asking,
and for a few days I could say no. We watched the sun go down
just before the solstice. "Sunsets don't make me sad," she said
each time we looked away from the Olympic Mountains.
"I'll be back soon," I told her.
"Yes," she said, as she always says.
"Yes, of course, take whatever you like."

II.

Fugit inreparabile tempus

Words you, too, have probably seen on sundials
and gravestones and mispronounced, helpless

human cohort, as you wander
the Museum of Useful Life.

On view now are rusted antennae filled with summer night,
and there's a vitrine for shoes beside a vitrine

for earthworms. "No building is . . . safe
unless the foundations lie six or seven feet

beneath the surface," wrote Darwin in 1881,
"at a depth at which worms cannot work."

The rule of thumb used to be that your grave
was supposed to be as deep as you are tall.

On a good day I'm 5'6",
which leaves me buried in a field of worms.

This was a very good day,
I wasn't thinking much about death,

though my friend was lying on a table across town
getting chemotherapy pumped uselessly into her veins.

It hasn't been working.
Not really.

Maybe not even at all.
I sat on a rock in the sun

and ate bread and cheese,
watching ants carry away more than their weight

of crumbs.
Truth is, I'm probably only 5'5" now,

what with the effects of gravity,
which is an incredibly useful force insofar as it keeps us

upright, attached to this earth.
It also lowers one of my eyelids

so men think I'm winking at them
though I'm not, this body is no longer

advertising. It gave birth to one child,
it traversed many miles.

I could try to argue that it deserves
a vitrine at the Museum,

but I'd rather come and go—
I'd rather be free,

as long as possible,
to come and go.

I thought about why God gave man free will.
And about the little microbes

feasting right there on our eyelashes.
What a job!

That's what my father would have said, were he still alive.
What use are his five children?

I can put in and take out a comma.
I can tell you to go look for places

in Paris where cracks in the sidewalk
have been filled in by an anonymous artist

who goes by the pseudonym Ememem,
which is the sound a moped makes.

Like some earthworms,
Ememem works only at night, he rides a moped

to wherever the city is breaking apart,
and replaces the missing pieces—

the cracks, potholes—
with mosaic grouted right into the gash.

He likes to be called "bitumen mender,"
"macadam surgeon," "poet of asphalt."

These are useful jobs: mender, surgeon.
Asphalt is useful, too,

made of liquid petroleum and small rocks.
But it can fall apart, like a body.

What more is there to say
than *fugit inreparibile tempus*?

Though rarely seen, earthworms
work best on these warm, damp nights.

Studies in Loneliness, iv

Plenty of time to be alone in the urn, the plastic bag. Scatter my ashes where? A sense of home could alleviate loneliness, I think, but where is home?

California? New York City? Alone in Canadensis?

Under that boulder I'd like to hire a crane to carry to my yard?

Right now it's waiting in the dirt field I pass as I drive uphill toward an unlit house.

—

We are so desperate to understand loneliness we've started experiment-ing on carpenter ants, who are a social bunch. To track them, scientists attached barcodes to the chitinous exoskeletons. Sometimes the barcodes fell off; sometimes one ant climbed on top of another, obfuscating vital statistics.

Ants accompanied by other ants lived about sixty days; the lone ants never stopped walking the perimeter of the enclosure, they never rested, apparently they were looking for the others, and they were unable to digest food,

not even sugar water could they digest.

This might explain why David's leg is always moving. He's a loner, as am I, and he's seeking even while he lies at midnight on the couch with the pellet stove on, looking into his books, into my eyes, into the flames that keep flaring up then going out for no known reason.

From above I imagine we, too, look like ants.

Think of those surveillance videos played back at high speed.

Ants shake right before they die. No great drama. And they do communicate, through their antennae, their pheromones.

———

Some of us write to appease the loneliness, why else leave a mark?

I was here, words say, this is what it was like, don't forget—

———

Could be that metaphors drawn from the human body make us feel more knowable: the tongue of our shoes, the eye of the storm.

Some people in their loneliness drink, imagining the bottle is a human mouth.

———

Show me not who you think I want you to be but who you are, Jamie's lover says, and I think this, were it possible, could be an antidote.

Art History

"I'm scared," Yayoi Kusama cried out,
"Somebody, please come."

This was the 1980s in New York City
and you know who lay beside her,

to soothe her? On Kawara,
who destroyed his painting

every night at midnight if he hadn't finished it yet.
"I am still alive!" he wrote in his telegrams,

which he considered works of art.
And they were,

and now he's not,
and now it's past midnight.

I haven't begun to finish.
Finish what?

The two mangoes that soften conspicuously?
Going through my papers? This draft?

In class I told my students,
"Listen, I'm not the Doctor of Clarity."

But I am trying to be clear—
On Kawara is no longer alive.

The city air smells like urine.
We are each one of us autonomous

nervous systems of yearning.
Last year I stood in a long line to enter

Yayoi Kusama's *Infinity Mirrored Room*,
a darkened 10' x 12' room lined with mirrors,

strung with LED lights and acrylic balls,
and for my allotted time

I saw myself repeated into infinity,
which is different from the task at hand,

which is to accept finitude.
I have two irises, two nipples, a first,

a middle, and a last name—
it's not like I've ever wished for more.

I have no trouble tossing out the shishito peppers
or the drycleaner's handwritten tag

with an ex's name still flashing its safety pin.
(I kept the safety pin.)

Was it climbing the stairs that kept me
from Kusama's other room, *Longing for Eternity*?

Or was it a question of time?
This year I didn't even have time for Valentine's Day,

though I liked looking around at all the little dogs
in their rubber booties, and all the passing faces,

some of which surely will be models for paintings
no one buys at estate sales that seem more frequent now.

Terribly frequent.
I am still alive!

And the estate liquidators keep flooding my inbox.
Some charge a flat-rate fee,

others work by percentages
and let you choose your own date.

Put me down for not yet.
Like everyone else, I didn't want to leave

the *Infinity Room*, the guard knocks
and says it's time to go, while upstairs

the line usually moves more quickly.
From what I can tell, *Longing for Eternity*

is not an immersive experience,
you just peek in, there is no god.

There is no guard to accompany you,
no guide to ferry you along.

Still Life

I can't hear them but I know
these peaches are breathing

here on the table, skins
touching in the bowl.

Even fruit exhales carbon dioxide,
as I'm doing now, trying to slow my pulse

after a small hapless blood clot
came to rest in the lungs

of a young woman who stopped by my office
with questions,

with her own steady exhalations.
But how?

How does a peach breathe?
The pit is so hard.

I hope she was not alone.
I hope she did not die alone.

I've been told I flail my arms
when I sleep, as if I were drowning.

As if I were waving. Here, here I am!
Tragedy makes me desperate

to acknowledge all I love.
"I love loneliness," I told a woman

who'd just read my tarot cards,
but the emptiness left by a death

is another species of loneliness
altogether. Unquantifiable

flailing beneath the meninges.
Every peach in every market

in every country of the world
is exhaling now. Peaches,

wine, bodies—these too I love.
You could circle the earth

with the veins, capillaries, and arteries
of anyone you've ever known

or never dreamed would die.
Then circle it again—

60,000 miles laid end to end.
Vessels, thresholds, life force,

ruins—these too I love,
immeasurably.

Reproducing at astonishing rates,
fruit flies feed on nectar, plant sap,

decaying fruit. I watch them gather
on the bowl of peaches in my room.

What room?
To make a room you fill it with rooms.

With loneliness.
With the voices and names of the dead.

Her name was April.
As if the body were a metaphor, she said.

Village of Dolls, i

Some people say Tsukimi Ayano makes her life-sized dolls
out of loneliness. I don't know what materials she uses—

foam, horsehair—or where the clothes come from, the hats.
She was born in Nagoro, moved away, came back

to a village with only thirty-some people living there.
The birds were pecking the vegetables in her father's garden.

She made a scarecrow so like him the neighbors passing by said,
"You're up early."

That was the first doll.
To replenish the village she made several hundred more,

slowly, it took years.
Like my mother greeting the agapanthus each morning,

Ayano speaks to the dolls who don't speak back,
dolls who don't last as long as most humans

and other readymades. Three years max.
She dresses them in waterproof clothes.

There are no more children in the village,
her dolls sit at the desks now, or stand

at the blackboard in the pose of teaching.
They also fish, repair roads, wait for the bus, doze.

She places them at the entrance to the valley.
Valley of the shadow of what?

The faces are the hardest part to make.
"I pull the string at the mouth and they smile," she says.

Three thousand years ago, the first scarecrows were live
children who ran through fields.

Studies in Loneliness, v

At the museum an Italian folk band started playing right beneath the big clock, young people pressed together in the central hall, arms raised, singing. Beside me a young man and a young woman were kissing. I filmed the crowd and felt dissolved into a kind of tidal bliss not unlike the intoxication of loneliness that leads us to the canvas, the keyboard, the blank page.

––––

Why paint a picture of a cow scratching himself against a tree?

Why was Degas so obsessed with the lacuna between audience and stage?

Why does Sophie Calle like small doors in big places, and how long did she live there, in the old Paris railway station, stealing things, rescuing notes from the trash?

––––

Sometimes, when their ambitions seem misdirected, I ask my students: "What is it books have done for you that you might wish your book would do for another?"

Were I to answer my own question: company in the void.

––––

Donna gave me a scarf silkscreened with a page from Virginia Woolf's diary. I can sleep beneath it, or fold it into a small soft stone upon which to lay my head.

"Greetings! my dear ghost."

Actuarial

Have you ever seen them,
the mortality tables?
Charts, graphs, years, dice.
Get back home, I tell myself.

Just as I'm telling you now.
It's good to get home
and slip back into bed,
thank the body beside you there,

or inside you once, or still,
or knocking gently at the door
until you say "come in."
No one knocks here in my office.

The thin gray carpet will outlast
foot traffic and fire.
Look, it's already so late—
I've turned every switch on

and it's still dark.
One lamp is made of alabaster,
it fills the room with a cold diffuse light,
and the stone stays cold to the touch.

I touch the shade to stay awake.
Piled on the desk like this, the charts stare
back up at me, and the numbers
begin to look like what I imagine

maggots to be, peristaltic telescoping
movements, barely ontological.
Sometimes I get so tired,
and afraid, I lie down right here.

I lie down on the dirty carpet,
the tables gathered
into a makeshift cushion
beneath a folded sweater.

At home, I have no carpets,
just floors installed inhabitants ago.
To keep the wood from splintering,
I use whatever I can find:

electrical tape, duct tape—
it all spools out so quickly.

The Specious Present

I stared at the tiny xeroxed faces
we wore like blurry jokes
pinned to our lapels.

Outside, the light raked the dry brown foothills
we slid down on flattened cardboard boxes,
decades ago, out of control, fast,

fast as years.
I still love the California hills,
I still love boxes and the way a word

is a box. It holds things,
flotsam holding flotsam.
Be the void, said the strobe-light disco ball.

The red wine warmed in my hands, it
spilled on my bare feet as I danced
above the San Andreas Fault.

"Cathy," they called me that night,
and in the reunion's obsolete blear
I looked a little like a Cathy,

or a Nadia, unrecognizable save for the eyes
and the animal drive to throw herself
into a long line of aerial cartwheels,

propelled forward and upside down
past language into anachronistic light.

Ars Poetica

All summer we played hide-and-seek
under the eucalyptus.

I liked all the games, their repetitions,
their songs.

Mother may I?
Simon says.

I couldn't wait to call *ollie ollie oxen free*,
sounds I loved not only for sound—

All summer we played hide-and-seek
under the eucalyptus tree.

Studies in Loneliness, vi

My aunts said they were worried about me when they heard how much I loved Beckett, whose prose I discovered on a friend's bookshelf in Tucson after walking barefoot across town drinking tequila. I knew I could simply copy Beckett's run-on sentences by hand for the rest of my life and feel I'd been understood and even that I'd made something.

–––

Beckett on Proust: ". . . we are alone. We cannot know and we cannot be known."

–––

I heat up the cast-iron pan before searing a steak for my mother, which my mother often did for my father.

I see her face and am afraid of the day it will no longer exist.

–––

The face is a loneliness inhaler! Which means:

a) it inhales loneliness
b) it's medicine for loneliness (taken as needed for rapid short-term relief of symptoms)

–––

This is what I'd like to get done in the next twenty-four hours: write twelve recommendations, type up all my notes on loneliness, try to say what it's like to be trapped as we are in an unmarked car traveling at high speeds down unknown roads, ostensibly at the wheel but really only a child inside saying slow down slow down.

It can be good to wash yourself in loneliness, rinse your body in it, pat a little of it on your crow's feet.

"Slow down," we'd beg our father, who never listened to our protests.

Not to be listened to is one of many fast-acting catalysts for loneliness.

Why not try?

Try to be known, try to say everything,

try to say what you need to say.

For the simple ongoing problem of I and thou, Hammacher Schlemmer sells a two-way live-conversation translator for $199.95 and, more reasonably, an LED face mask that flashes a kaleidoscopic light show across what the copywriters call "your mouth hole."

(Satisfaction guaranteed.)

So many of these words have been used by others.

So many of these shoes have been worn by others. I hope to return them eventually, for others to wear. Even these suede ones resting lightly now on the stretcher of the empty chair beside me here at Malecon, where I just heard Danny died. He was a regular, like Lucy and Will and David and Pedro; they're all in the group portrait hanging on the central wall.

I'm not in that scene, but I'm here, too, unframed and on my own, just beside the others, my likeness suspended on a nail above the window table, a little askew.

Sometimes, when he's home, my son joins me here and we do our work quietly together.

—

I want responsibility for as little as possible, not even a ficus plant. Basil, ok.

Best not to get too attached.

Boom!

Sudden glimpse of the human predicament: spotlight on the center ring where loneliness is the net beneath the trapeze act of love.

Or is it the other way round?

—

I often fall asleep on the living room couch beside an enormous stack of papers, not far from a drawer of cotton sheets I will not live long enough to use.

Somehow men seem to be getting older, the younger ones, I mean, which is a kind of pleasure, the cortical hubs light up. They light up when I touch this man's cashmere sweater here by the loud fish tank.

In a blue garbage bag, the chickens marinate on their skewers.

The newscaster is wearing a pink dress with crablike epaulettes.

Outside, a yellow-slickered cop and her whistle are heading uptown.

If you could describe this world, would that be a stay against loneliness?

Ash on my winter hat.

Critique of Pure Reason

With him pressed so close beside her,
she couldn't sleep. Perhaps it was his skin,
or the rain. It kept raining.

She lay there trying to remember
exactly how many thoughts she could have.
Was it 30,000 or 70,000? Per hour?

Or was it per minute?
She'd heard from someone
who'd heard from someone

who heard the number, whatever it was,
from an HVAC specialist.
She placed his hand back on her chest

while another fifty thoughts leaked out.
They'd both been reading César Aira,
who said that for every sentence you write

there are many implicit questions.
She was surprised to find herself still wearing
the shirt he'd pulled down from the neck

to reach the rest of her. The shirt
was like a second skin, color of her nipples.
Pale burgundy. It held her together,

kept her from flying right out of her body.
His T-shirt had a hole, a tear near the hem,
which she only later remembered noticing.

Fingering.
How many other thoughts had she had
while her body was responding like that?

She didn't know if pleasure counted as thought,
or were they separate categories.
The smell of someone lingered.

Or was it cilantro? The insoles
of the red shoes in her bedroom?
Secondhand. They were like ballet shoes

though she was not a dancer.
The fact of the shoes elicits hundreds
or thousands of thoughts,

and if she could just keep writing
at top speed she'd be able to count them.
She can type 120 words a minute,

and let's say a thought averages fifteen words:
she could type approximately 480 thoughts every hour.
With a pen she writes more slowly.

To whom is she writing?
Over a small glass of whiskey she'd asked
what was the most debauched he'd ever been.

"Dropping acid with a friend," he said.
She didn't tell him about lying on the floor
half-naked with the red ballet shoes beside her

in an apartment not far from the cathedral
the night someone drove a truck at high speed
down the crowded sidewalk.

Those shoes—those thoughts—
How quickly they move
across the 90,000 miles of neurons

packed into her head. How long
had the shoes been worn by someone else
before she wore them?

Isn't there something morbid about that?
Or is it like taking psilocybin,
you realize everyone is connected,

the near and the far?
Even if it all ends tomorrow,
she'll have been grateful he awakened her.

She'd come to expect a life without much pleasure
other than rain and sleep and solitude
and whatever she could make in her notebook

and in the narrow galley kitchen buffeted by cabinets
filled with glass jars and oils and a canister of propane
in case of emergency.

The overhead light has been out for years.
Why? Why can't she climb the ladder,
unscrew the bulbs, fix the wiring?

She found him sitting quietly at the kitchen table
where she could smell the basil she'd watched
him tear into small pieces the night before:

basil and sun and man: and then she wiped
a few grains of coffee from the counter
into the other irreducible qualia of morning.

Village of Dolls, ii

Did I just dream the dolls take part
in a big game of tug-of-war? Or did I
hear it on the radio I keep turned down so low

I can fall asleep to human discourse
without having to comprehend the meaning?
I haven't played tug-of-war in years

but I remember the pulse of eros
through the rope and the heap
we fell into on either end.

There were so many of us then,
and even more now. Some of us
insist on smiling, others on kneeling.

"I don't think dying is scary," the artist says.
"I'll probably live forever."

Awe

Celebratory,
gently onomatopoetic,

almost indecorous, the words a pleasure
to repeat—everyone said it,

"the whole shebang"—
but if what Skeat said was true, if *shebang* first meant

"temporary shelter," if all of
it is only temporary . . .

I didn't like to think about it.
Beneath the blue whale,

at the Museum of Natural History,
I understood I was a small lone figure swept up in waves.

The whale wore 600 pounds of paint.
I wore waterproof mascara and Geox,

the metal eyelets flickering
beneath her ten tons.

I wore those shoes everywhere
but did not wear through their breathable

membrane, which someone thought to patent.
Isn't it wonderful that the soles

breathe, like all animals?
Like the speechless human animal

bending now to double-knot the laces
as the black sneakers collect dust,

the dust of exhalation.
Exultation.

It seemed everything was breathing,
even the blue skylights with their blue bulbs,

the passersby in the vast family hall.
Beneath her body we walked beside other bodies,

we walked away, we planned to return,
safe in our temporary chambers.

III.

Studies in Loneliness, vii

We come to know who we are, says Emmanuel Levinas, by looking into another's face.

―

When I teach, I seem to let all twelve hearts beat inside my own. No wonder it's both an opiate and a weight.

Does a heart adjust to other hearts in the room, the way our periods synchronize, the way I hold my head mirroring yours? Whoever you are.

―

Helen says a difference in expectation applies to every sexual encounter. It wasn't so long ago that I spent the winter reading Apollinaire's letters waiting for a man who seemed to say it was over simply by removing one of the many hairs that cling to whatever I wear.

―

Someone is shuffling through me, moving the hanger along to look at the other blouses and sweaters, and sometimes the clock starts beating inside my heart, and then there's even more noise, mortal noise.

Unoccupied Time

The line at the market
moved so slowly it's possible
my vagina shrunk to the size
of a fingernail.

That's what the tabloid said could happen,
and I was so suggestible
I felt it was true.
I read the whole issue,

which OK wasn't Derrida or
Cornel West but did give me a few
ideas, unstoppable rhizomes,
wolf men, gold rush,

the return of the seventeen-year
cicada. The sheer life force of a weed
named hairy bittercress, which flings
its seeds three feet into the air.

Life force . . .
There was a boulder at the foot of the hill,
which I wanted somehow to haul up to my place.
The Coptic monks had said yes,

I could have it, but it was so heavy.
Pure dead weight. Igneous
or sedimentary, I didn't know.
I didn't want to die alone.

Kody said he'd borrow a rig
and once the ground dried out
he'd tow it to me, where
did I want it placed,

in the shade by the spruce
or in full sun? One more thing
I couldn't decide. Some tombstone.
Logic said if I was in line

at the 24/7 grocery store then I wasn't
alone, I was waiting with others,
the lights would be on, surveillance
cameras fired up, other people

too must be waiting and breathing,
like my friend, who was waiting
for news from the doctor. Without
ever saying so, each of us had promised

to be there for and after the other's
death, which defies logic. I wasn't
going to cry, neither of us were.
To pass the time, I opened

another tabloid and saw it was
possible to plant old ginger,
like the kind I had in my cart,
I loved ginger, I was buying extra

to ease my friend's nausea. The little eyes
would sprout. They would regrow and
rise up and see everything
heal and form calluses.

In Utero and After

I just learned that the perforation of the mouth
happens at four weeks.

You here beside me, decanting spirits
into your own perforation,

did you know that?
I don't drink much

but seem somehow to have ordered
a shot of amniotic fluid.

Everything's a little milky in this strange light.
It's too dark here to study the obituaries,

we can always do that later, in my bed,
where it's a little warmer.

Do you mind my asking
if you might like to come home with me,

when this is over? Or better yet, before then?
I can feel my own mouth opening and closing

like the mouth of a fish,
about to ask what we're doing here,

what kind of theater is this.
Not the local vet's office

where just yesterday the surgeon said
my dog had no more lady parts

and handed them over in formaldehyde.
Formaldehyde! What a drink.

Mine too has been a brief fertile cameo,
and maybe yours has, too, a cameo

worth repeating.
Stay with me, won't you, while the bartender

pours a little more of everything
into the decanter—

eros eros eros
brief, brief

Ars Poetica

"What can I know? What ought I to do?
What may I hope? What is the human being?"
—Immanuel Kant

To answer Kant's last question she should take the curtains from her eyes
and lay them on the bed.

She should stand on her head and dream,
empty herself of *I, I, I, I.*

She should walk inside the living and the dead,
become some other passerby.

Studies in Loneliness, viii

From the 725 results found using the keyword "lonely" in the search engine at the Metropolitan Museum of Art's website, updated nightly:

The Artist, Seated in front of a Dolmen (Johan Thomas Lundbye, 1844, work on paper)

Boundlessly Free and Content (Hashimoto Dokuzan, early 20th century, hanging scroll, ink on paper)

A Figure Resting in a Ruined Tower (John Sell Colman, 1810–1840, graphite)

The Great Sirens (Paul Delvaux, 1947, oil on masonite)

Hope for the Future (Charles Wilbert White, 1945, lithograph)

Into the World There Came a Soul Called Ida (Ivan Albright, 1940, lithograph)

Limestone statue of a bearded man with votive offering (Cypriot, c. 475–450 BCE, limestone)

The Lone Pine (Anne W. Brigman, c. 1908, gelatin silver print)

Lone Traveler in Wintry Mountains (Yosa Buson, c. 1778, folding screen)

The Lost Mind (Elisha Vedder, 1865, oil on canvas)

Lovers' Double Grave (Kobayakawa Shūsei, 1920s, hanging scroll, ink on paper)

Marvelous Verses without Sound (Xiao Yuncong, c. 1660–1673, ink and color on paper)

Night Shadows (Edward Hopper, 1921, etching)

Reliquary (Italian, 15th century, silver and enamel)

The Sound of Spring in a Lonely Valley (Hongren, 1661, hanging scroll, ink on paper)

Valentine, "remember me" (anonymous, c. 1880, cameo-embossed open-work lace paper)

Where but to think is to be full of sorrow

Security confiscated the bracelet I'd slipped
into my wallet but not the thin black sweater
I wore as I walked out of Macy's.
The sweater still had its price tag

and was so soft it soothed whoever was whispering
"more, more" in my ears adorned with silver hoops
no one thought to question me about.
Decades later, I still have it—

the urge to steal things I might someday put to use.
Tiny plastic bottles filled with oil and vinegar.
Matches. Mechanical pencils, endlessly refillable,
can never be used up and still I want more.

Down at the local Bartell's,
two years to the day after my father died
and they zipped him into a bag
and carried him out before dawn,

I slid one slim blue BIC from its packaging
and sat there on the drugstore floor
trying to fix the thing,
trying to fix the thing I'm always working on.

What belongs to whom, who gets taken
from whom, and how, how it happens.
I wasn't thinking only about my father.
I was thinking about my father's

tenet that most anything can be solved
if you think hard enough about it.
Following no logic but the hand's,
I copied Keats's words into my notebook,

in .5 mm soft lead, and again here,
across this sheet of unlined paper.
Because the blood vessels in his brain
had hardened. Because at the moment

he stopped breathing—and in the months before
and never since—I had held his hand.
At 11 p.m.
At 11 p.m. there are far too many

and far too few hours until daylight.
It was so quiet I couldn't help but
hear myself think of my father's hands,
which had softened beautifully and terribly.

How to Prepare

Best not to dream of death as an enormous spider
crossing an empty highway. Instead imagine something
all your own to kiss and hug, and small hummingbirds
that look like azure foil. If you too awaken between
3:00 and 5:00 to stare into the abyss where flies gather,
call me, I'll talk you through until morning. If you sign
the release form, I can cite you in the study.
Release, yes, that's the term I was looking for.
Shake your nightclothes out well.
The human condition is made of moisture and heat.
So far, my research is very ad hoc, like dreaming.
I lay my head on the pillow by itself and press "record."
Some of us will die alone in our sleep. Peacefully.
Because I know I talk in my sleep, I hope one day
to transcribe these recordings, and the sound of children
passing now by the open window.

Triumph of Dionysos and the Seasons

I don't want to find myself being choked
by binocular straps slipped over my head
and around my neck. But were it to happen,

I know not to show fear, far better to ask
the stranger matching his steps to mine
about the ducks floating on the lake,

or the clouds in the sky, ask anything to show
with your questions you're not afraid,
you don't understand what's happening,

which is easy for me, no need to feign
not-understanding, it follows me, even to the Met
where there are no remote trails around no lake.

Nothing to be afraid of.
All of us hurrying
past the Roman sarcophagus

with its final inscription not yet carved
into the marble. Upstairs,
Alice Neel is naked, staring out at us

from a late, unsparing self-portrait,
holding a brush in her right hand.
"What's that patch of blue?" I asked the guard

who kept me from getting too close.
I wanted to see how it was done,
how she painted scars and betrayal and loss

and the bowl of fruit, the clear glass bottle
from a New York that no longer exists.
"Visiting a museum is a matter of going from void to void,"

said Robert Smithson, whose spirit Neel captured
in a portrait that will, like everything in the show,
like everyone studying the "awful dichotomies"

mentioned in the museum placards,
be removed, replaced by something
equally beautiful.

On canvas, Smithson is still a young man,
he hadn't yet died, hadn't yet hauled 6,000 tons
of black basalt and local soil to the Great Salt Lake

where he spread the organic and inorganic materials
into a spiral that disappears and reappears
from its useless berm.

Walking by, a woman looked up at him and said,
"I don't like his face." But I did.
I liked even her face,

I liked all the faces I saw,
faces that would soon or had already become
diatomaceous earth.

How crowded the museum was,
and cool, so cool my red summer dress—
still sweaty from my having rushed across the park

tracked by dread, traffic, time, digitized
to a small blue circle circling the reservoir,
the reservoir with its merganser ducks,

its laughing summer gulls—
was like my own skin, weightless and damp
and cold, when a stranger,

mistaking me for someone else,
or taking a shine to my silver braid,
my mottled calves, matched his steps to mine

and without a word pressed his hand gently
against my lower back. Gently.
There was no reason to be reassured.

I couldn't shake him.
I couldn't shake the feeling of him.
Like that, we walked side by side,

hurrying up and slowing down, into the last gallery,
"The Human Comedy," the words stenciled
directly onto the far wall.

I might have thought to ask if he'd read Balzac
or Dante. I should have asked.
I couldn't shake him.

Or I couldn't shake the feeling of him.
I could hear his shoes tapping the cool museum floor.
I could feel his hand steady against my back,

like the touch of an assailant
or a shepherd, I didn't ask which.

Studies in Loneliness, ix

Which is to say what you already know through experience: that lone-liness happens even in the midst of people.

That possessions are a common placebo.

That my dining room table faces a wall of books.

"Could anyone be lonely with all these books?" I ask my son, who likes silence more than I do.

—

Everything that gets expelled is strange,

even a child.

Spit, tears, blood, breath.

—

Seems we are afloat in an ocean of estrangement, ever since that first expulsion, so I activate my mirror neurons, which activate my brow, which furrows into lines they call the "elevens." The dermatologist says I would have more positive reinforcement were I to get rid of my elevens.

Do I look angry, or just sad?

I am sad, my mother will soon die. We bathed with her, we slept be-side her—

—

I keep buying secondhand cashmere sweaters because wearing cashmere makes me feel as if I'm wearing another human body.

Sometimes I try to soothe myself by repairing things.

Marie resoled a pair of shoes four times before the cobbler said, "Marie, I think that's about it."

Having supplies can seem like an antidote to loneliness, which might explain why I filled my basement with cereal and lightbulbs.

I don't want to know what it's like underground.

Is this why we have dogs leashed to us? Children? Things? Lines once heard we can't forget—

Back out of all this now too much for us

The moon is my mother

In a package of minutes there is this We

Thought Experiment

What would it be like to be a mantis shrimp,
poorly understood, territorial, combative,

with part of your brain housed
in each eyestalk?

I don't think it's exactly love, but some species
are monogamous, sharing a patch of sea grass

or underwater burrow for twenty years.
My place is probably 150 feet above sea level

and when my son comes back home, he sleeps
in his old captain's bed above his old T-shirts.

Sometimes he brings his dog,
a rescue, and calls me Dogma,

then they're gone again
and I rattle around again, mindlessly,

listening to my neighbor sing.
From the far end of the galley kitchen

I can watch the Hudson tides rise and fall,
can imagine being dredged in a net

dropped by the sloop my son and his classmates
sailed, long ago, when they were still children.

I remember looking out the window then, too,
watching the *Clearwater*

make its leisurely way up and back.
Was my mind already housed here in my eyes,

which, like all human eyes, like to close—
to rest, dream, recall a face, a child's voice

who is no longer a child? Who knows
what else they're thinking about now.

True story about the mantis shrimp
who shattered her aquarium walls.

Because she was alone?
Or because she was not alone enough?

Stories I cannot tell because I don't know
how they end and might never understand.

Who would buy a mantis shrimp,
lifted from the sea grass,

sent by express mail to be dropped
into a thousand distant aquariums

where she swivels her compound eyes
and takes everything in.

Restricted Fragile Materials

It should be easy, I tell my son,
to dispose of the possessions kept
in these rooms.

I've left some things on a shelf for him, see?
These coupons might still be valid,
the vinegar will keep forever.

I've always liked the idea of order.
I've always liked the idea of the sofa at West Elm
but never did commit.

If I could, I'd just lie here
taking measurements,
leaving ghostlier and ghostlier

impressions until thinking ends
and the lights go out.
Let my memory-depleted memory

preserve all this joy:
restricted fragile materials.
Who can stop me?

It's not illegal to want to hold on.
To get to my archives,
my son will have to put his ear to the ground,

listen for a quiet scream.
And beneath that, like groundwater,
the endless chatter

of praise and lament.
How will I tell him the river I
feared to drink from

has come to drink from me?
May he, too, have fair winds
and following seas.

Studies in Loneliness, x

Lying at the edge of her bed, my friend was trying to stay alert.

I had promised to be with her when she died, as she had promised to be with me.

Every day for eighteen months I thought she might die. Often I thought she already had; I'd wait for her chest to rise, as it was doing even more sparingly.

———

The bedside table was a compendium of pills; there was dust on the lip of the vase, on the mechanical pencils. I refilled her glass with cold water. She liked to drink from tiny glasses, I don't why.

It gave me something to do, filling them over and over as lucidity grew further out of her reach. Somehow she'd made it to her son's birthday, to her birthday. Soon she would be asleep again. "It will be so strange not to have you here," she said.

Words said more frequently as May and then the end of May approached. The only other sound in the room was the fan, the ice stirring in the glass as she took a sip of the cold cold water she craved. Her door was open to the kitchen and I could hear the cubes falling with abandon from the freezer into its small collection bin. My plane was leaving in thirty-six hours.

I don't know if she was asking me to stay.

Who held whose gaze?

Her caregiver realigned her almost translucent body to make her more comfortable. "What about that . . . ?" she said, looking back at me. "For a title, I mean."

She didn't have to explain. I knew what she meant. I had wished aloud for a solution for the problem of bodies in space, wanting to be in two places at the same time. There, and here.

I was gathering my things. "I like it," I said, "but does the book have enough to do with—"

"Everything," she said with quiet clarity from behind a wall of methadone, oxycontin, lorazepam.

I think she was already in two places at the same time.

———

When my afternoons became her mornings, everywhere I looked I saw someone had tried to solve the problem. There were the bridges that cross the Arno, frescoes in San Marco. There was dust in the open sarcophagus. Dionysos in long hair. There should have been the phone but there were only opiates, which made it impossible by then to reach her.

———

Every day I put on my pale blue sneakers and tie the laces and then I find myself outside.

———

To get to the outskirts of town, I had to take a subterranean passage under the train tracks and keep going. I understood I should keep going until I stood before a door. It was cool and rainy. Unseasonably cool for Florence. Unseasonably lonely.

I rang the bell and waited. There was still time to catch my breath, there was still time to lay my body down and let Luca begin to touch me.

Then slowly I walked back to my rented apartment a different way: over the tracks, on a footbridge that floated above it all.

I had not planned to undergo research here, *al di fuori*, so far away, while it was happening.

Dusk. Soon it will be the longest day of the year.

NOTES

"Studies in Loneliness, i": Thanks to writers Leigh Newman and Hannah Tinti for the conversation that first got me thinking about the value of loneliness to a writer's life.

Carson McCullers's story "A Tree. A Rock. A Cloud." is from her 1951 collection, *The Ballad of the Sad Café*.

The statistic about loneliness in schoolchildren is noted, among other places, in Olympia Palikara, Susana Castro-Kemp, Carolina Gaona, and Vasiliki Eirinaki, "The mediating role of school belonging in the relationship between socioemotional well-being and loneliness in primary school age children," *Australian Journal of Psychology*, 73:1, 24–34, 2021.

Margot Guralnick's found art can be seen in galleries and on Instagram at dogwalkdiarynyc.

"Envoy": Abraham H. Maslow (1908–1970) introduced the idea of a "hierarchy of needs" in his study "A Theory of Human Motivation," published in *Psychological Review* in 1943: "Man is a perpetually wanting animal. Also no need or drive can be treated as if it were isolated or discrete; every drive is related to the state of satisfaction or dissatisfaction of other drives."

"Nicholson Baker & I": Nicholson Baker is the author of more than fifteen books, including *The Anthologist, U&I: A True Story*, and *A Box of Matches*.

"Itinerary": Bulova's Accutron Spaceview wristwatch was manufactured from 1960 to 1976 and relied on a small tuning fork that created a humming sound.

Gordon Cooper was an American astronaut, engineer, and test pilot. He spent thirty-four hours in his spacecraft *Faith 7*, orbiting the earth; he was the first American to sleep in space and the last American to fly a solo orbital mission.

"'Have You Ever Written a Poem about Death?' My Mother Asks": William Carlos Williams's poem "Death" was first published in the journal *Blues* in 1930.

"The Search": *Ethical Theory: Classical and Contemporary Readings* (Louis P. Pojman, ed., Wadsworth Publishing, 1989); the cited quote is from *The Roots of Romanticism*, Isaiah Berlin, ch. 1, "In Search of a Definition."

"Untitled": There is a direct allusion to—a respectful misquotation of—Emily Dickinson's poem [479 (Franklin)], "Because I could not stop for Death –."

"*Fugit inreparabile tempus*": The title of this poem is a familiar expression drawn from Virgil's *Georgics*, book 3, line 284. It translates as: "It escapes, irretrievable time."

The quote from Charles Darwin is from his publication *The formation of vegetable mould through the action of worms, with observations on their habits* (London: John Murray, 1881).

"Studies in Loneliness, iv": The research on carpenter ants was reported in Akiko Koto, Danielle Mersch, Brian Hollis, and Laurent Keller, "Social isolation causes mortality by disrupting energy homeostasis in ants," *Behavioral Ecology and Sociobiology*, 69, 583–591 (2015).

"Art History": Conceptual artist On Kawara (1932–2014) began his Date Paintings in January 1966; there are almost 3,000 in the series. His *I Am Still Alive* series was begun in 1969 and lasted for more than thirty years (until telegrams became obsolete). The telegrams were sent to friends, artists, curators, and acquaintances.

The two Yayoi Kusama artworks mentioned here are at the Broad, in Los Angeles.

"Still Life": In memoriam, April Freely.

"Village of Dolls, i": Nagoro is a small village in Japan's Iya Valley (on the island of Shikoku, Tokushima Prefecture) that artist Tsukimi Ayano has filled with dolls.

The poem alludes to Psalms 23:4.

"Studies in Loneliness, v": The artworks mentioned here include Constant Troyon's 1859 *Vache qui se gratte*; Edgar Degas's many paintings of ballet dancers on stage; and Sophie Calle's 2022 exhibition at the Musée d'Orsay, *Les Fantômes d'Orsay.*

"Greetings! my dear ghost" is from Virginia Woolf's diary, 9 March 1920.

"Actuarial": There is an admiring nod to Yusef Komunyakaa's "Ode to the Maggot" here.

"The Specious Present": The term "specious present" was coined by E. Robert Kelly in the nineteenth century and later elaborated on by William James.

Dr. Dog's seventh album *Be the Void* was released in 2012. The group was performing in Seattle at the Neptune Theater in 2020, and "Be the Void" flyers were affixed to the city's lampposts and traffic lights.

"Nadia" refers to the gymnast Nadia Comăneci.

"Studies in Loneliness, vi": The Samuel Beckett quote is drawn from his 1930 essay on Marcel Proust.

The portraits referred to in the poem were painted by Manny Vega; born 1956 in the Bronx, Vega's work hangs not only at Malecon but also in museums, galleries, and the New York subway system. With thanks to everyone at Malecon, including Anna, Cathy, Eduardo, Fatima, Fernando, Francisco, Franklin, Gladys, Moreno, Nana, Nancy, Neno, Orlando, Pablo, Ramon, Rolando, Sarah, and Yazzi.

"Critique of Pure Reason": The title is taken from Immanuel Kant's 1781 metaphysical study by the same name.

"Awe": Walter W. Skeat, *An Etymological Dictionary of the English Language.*
This poem's last line echoes Emily Dickinson's "Safe in their Alabaster Chambers −" [124 (Franklin)].

"*Where but to think is to be full of sorrow*": The title of this poem is a line from John Keats's "Ode to a Nightingale."

"*Triumph of Dionysos and the Seasons*": This poem opens with a reference to one of the essays in Maggie O'Farrell's *I Am, I Am, I Am: Seventeen Brushes with Death.*

The Roman sarcophagus *Triumph of Dionysos and the Seasons* is on view in the Greek and Roman halls at the Metropolitan Museum of Art.

Alice Neel's paintings were exhibited at the Metropolitan Museum in 2021. "The awful dichotomies" is a term borrowed from an interview with Neel, who spoke about the tension between mothering and making art.

The sculptor Robert Smithson's quote is drawn from his essay "Some Void Thoughts on Museums," published in *Robert Smithson: The Collected Writings*.

"Studies in Loneliness, ix" : Lines quoted from Robert Frost's "Directive," Sylvia Plath's "The Moon and the Yew Tree," and Gwendolyn Brooks's "An Aspect of Love, Alive in the Ice and Fire."

"Restricted Fragile Materials": This poem is in conversation with Nancy Kuhl, poet and curator at the Beinecke Rare Book and Manuscript Library at Yale University.

"Studies in Loneliness, x": In memoriam, Saskia Hamilton.

ACKNOWLEDGMENTS

I would like to thank the editors of the following journals and series for publishing these poems (sometimes in different versions or with different titles):

> The Academy of American Poets' Poem-a-Day Series,
> "The Specious Present"
> *The American Poetry Review*, "Envoy," "*Fugit inreparabile tempus*,"
> "Untitled," "*Triumph of Dionysos and Apollo*"
> *Freeman's*, "Itinerary"
> *Harper's Magazine*, "Village of Dolls, i"
> *The Nation*, "Night Watch"
> *The New York Review of Books*, "Morning of Departure"
> *The New Yorker*, "Hyacinth" and "Thought Experiment"
> *The Yale Review*, "Nicholson Baker & I," "The Search,"
> "In Utero and After"

This is the least lonely part of the writer's life: the chance to thank the fellow travelers, writers, and friends who have, sometimes without realizing it, accompanied and eased the making of a book. To that end, I'd like to express my gratitude for the care and guidance shared with me by these remarkable people: Chris Baswell, Leslie Bushara, James Ciano, Cort Day, Rachel Eisendrath, Alexandra Enders, Miranda Field, Ed Hirsch, Marie Howe, Susan Karwoska, Donika Kelly, Nancy Kuhl, Ben Lerner, Rich McLaughlin, Fiona McCrae, Steven Mero, Laurel Morris, Michael Morse, John Murillo, Dennis Nurkse, Kathleen Peirce, Caryl Phillips, Karin Roffman, Julie Schnatz Rybeck, Helen Schulman, Nicole Sealey, Tom Sleigh, Timea Szell, Mary Szybist, Thierry Trubert, Jean Valentine (rest in peace), Ellen Bryant Voigt, and Elise Wiarda.

Several beloveds appear in these pages by first name; I thank you all.

And ongoing thanks to Claudia Rankine, who helps me minimize my maybes without minimizing essential forms of not-knowing; to Donna Masini and Jericho Brown, the closest of close readers; to Maureen N. McLane, whose pyrotechnic improvisations fill me with a sense of possibility; to Jen Grotz, Ilya Kaminsky, Deborah Landau, Geoffrey Nutter,

Maya C. Popa, and Abby Wender, for literary conversations that transcend the page and are essential to these pages; to David Wells, for his love of beauty and for his patient help; and to Saskia Hamilton, who even when she's no longer here is very much here with us and in these poems.

It's wonderful to be able to thank my students—past, present, future—whom I hope to fail only in the ways a teacher's limitations are useful, maybe even necessary, to a poet's true education.

Gratitude to my editor Jeff Shotts, for his inimitable way of both questioning and supporting as he helps a book find its shape and contents; to everyone at Graywolf, a press I admire for the way it honors both the life and the work of its writers; to the American Academy of Arts and Letters, the Guggenheim Foundation, and the Civitella Ranieri Foundation for their support.

For the unerring compass their love provides, it is a joy to thank my family: my son, my sisters, my brother, and my mother, whose creative drive and spirit have guided us all.

CATHERINE BARNETT is the author of three previous poetry collections: *Human Hours*; *The Game of Boxes*; and *Into Perfect Spheres Such Holes Are Pierced*. Her honors include a Guggenheim Fellowship, an Award in Literature from the American Academy of Arts and Letters, the Believer Book Award, the James Laughlin Award, the Beatrice Hawley Award, and a Whiting Award. She lives in New York City, where she works as an independent editor and teaches in the Creative Writing Program at NYU.

The text of *Solutions for the Problem of Bodies in Space*
is set in Bembo MT Pro.
Composition by Bookmobile Design & Digital
Publisher Services, Minneapolis, Minnesota.
Manufactured by Versa Press on acid-free,
30 percent postconsumer wastepaper.